Interactive Bible Stories for Children:

Old Testament

Group
Loveland, Colorado

Interactive Bible Stories for Children: Old Testament

Copyright © 1994 Group Publishing, Inc.

First Printing

Contributors
Lois Keffer, Martin Nagy, Amy Nappa, Beth Rowland, Joani Schultz, Janice Thatcher, Jennifer Root Wilger, and Christine Yount

Credits
Edited by Jennifer Root Wilger and Lois Keffer
Cover designed by Liz Howe
Interior designed by Lisa Smith
Illustrations by John Lee

Library of Congress Cataloging-in-Publication Data
Interactive Bible stories for children. Old Testament/[contributors, Lois Keffer. . . et al.].
    p.   cm.
  ISBN 1-55945-190-4
  1. Bible stories, English—O.T. [1. Bible stories—O.T.]
I. Keffer, Lois. II. Group Publishing.
BS551.2.I57 1994
221.9'505—dc20   93-41548
                                                                        CIP
                                                                        AC

Printed in the United States of America

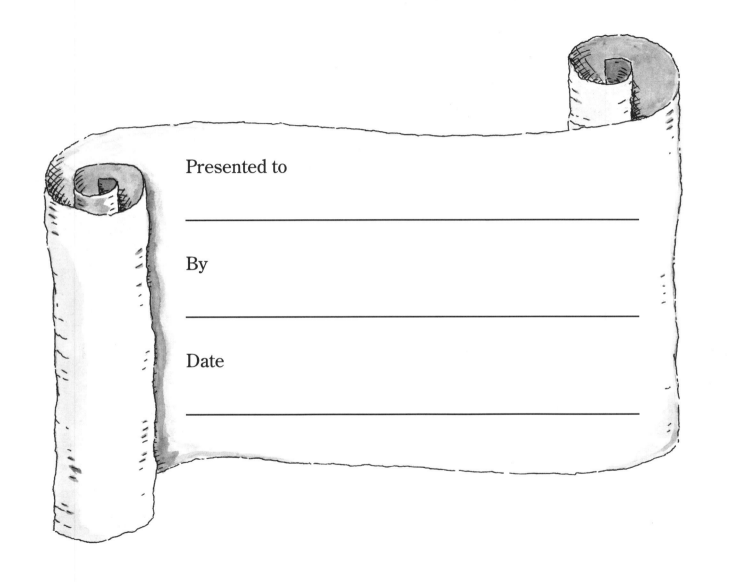

Presented to

By

Date

Contents

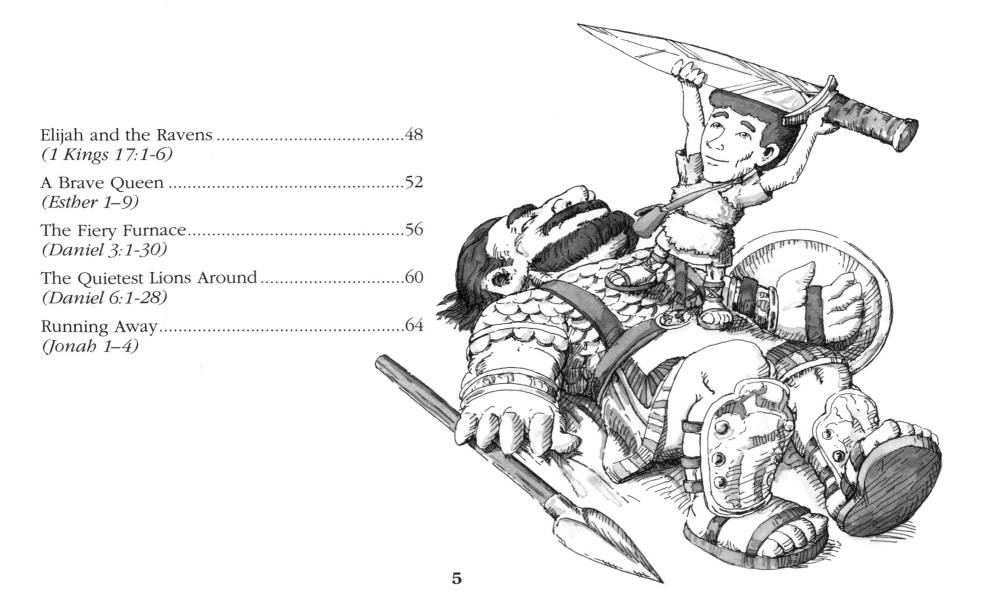

Introduction

Bible stories are the very heart and fabric of our Christian faith. They teach us about the heart of God. They show us the extent of God's love. They stretch our imagination, engage our emotions, and ignite our faith. It's never too soon to share the truth and wonder of the Bible with children.

Introducing children to Bible stories is both a wonderful privilege and a sacred trust. To young children, the storyteller embodies God's love and care. The excitement you feel as you share God's Word is contagious! As the old saying goes, "Faith is more often caught than taught."

Interactive Bible Stories for Children: Old Testament brings a delightfully fresh approach to sharing the Bible with children. You don't have to be a professional storyteller to teach these Bible stories in a memorable way. Interactive questions and motions draw children into the Bible and bring the stories to life. You'll actually experience the stories together as you read.

Each interactive Bible story is different. Your children will run from the Egyptians with Moses and the Israelites. They'll march around the city of Jericho with Joshua. They'll talk with you about what it would be like to be swallowed by a fish.

As you enjoy these stories together, kids will intertwine their own experiences with those of the Bible characters. As they learn about brave Queen Esther, they'll share times when they had to do something scary. They'll thank God for taking care of them as they see how God sent food to Elijah. Because they're involved in the story, children will remember and apply each story's message.

Interactive Bible Stories for Children: Old Testament is simple to use. Just choose a story, sit down with your children, and start to read. Interactive motions and questions are built right into the story. No advance preparation is required. You can use these stories with one or two children at home or with groups of children in a variety of church settings.

Here are some storytelling hints to help you get started:

Get down to your children's level. Sit on the floor or in a low chair. Read with enthusiasm. Don't forget to pause for children to discover details in the illustrations for each story. They'll enjoy looking for all the different animals that went into the ark and seeing how Jonah really did get swallowed by a big fish!

Follow the directions in each story. If the story says, "Let's march with Joshua," set the book down and pretend to march right along with the children. Children will welcome and follow your participation. So have fun!

Adapt the motions and questions to your listeners. Add more motions for younger children or more questions for older children. Use the motions and questions in the text as a springboard to get your children talking about the story.

Interactive Bible Stories for Children: Old Testament will make the Bible come alive for your children—and for you!

Best of all, you'll be doing your part to ensure that another generation will grow up knowing and loving the God of the Bible.

The Beginning of Everything

(From Genesis 1–2)

Before there was anything at all, there was God. God loves to make things. Do you like to make things? What's your favorite thing you've made?

Before God began making things, there was NOTHING! Close your eyes and cover them with your hands. What do you see? That's what it was like—only blackness.

Then God said, "Let there be light." And there was! Open your eyes.

God looked at the light and said, "That's good!" Every time you hear me say, "That's good," make a thumbs-up sign. Let's try that. "That's good!"

Next God made the sky. What do you see in the sky? Let's make our hands float across the sky like fluffy little clouds.

Then God made the land. Let's pat the ground. Then God made the sea! Let's use our arms and hands to make waves in the water. God was busy!

God looked at the beautiful, green land and the bright, blue sea and said, "That's good!"

Then God made things grow on the earth—grass and bushes and flowers and trees. Can you make your arms grow up like a tree? What kind of fruit grows on you?

God looked at the grass and bushes and flowers and trees and said, "That's good!"

Then God made the stars! Let's make twinkling stars by snapping our fingers in the air. What else is in the sky? God made that, too!

And God said, "That's good!"

Next God made living things for the seas. Who lives in the sea?

God made gobs of guppies and oodles of octopuses. He made piles of porpoises, millions of mussels, and billions of barnacles. The sea was full of slippery, flippery swimmers. Let's make our hands swim like fish.

God also made living things for the air. Flap, whir, whiz, buzz! What creatures did God make to live in the air? Let's fly like birds. Let's buzz like bees. Let's flutter down and land on a flower like a butterfly.

Next God made animals to live on the earth.

Oodles and oodles of animals. Creepy, crawly creatures; fuzzy, furry creatures; slippery, slimy creatures; and wiggly, wet creatures. Slow creatures, fast creatures, great big and small creatures.

God made all creatures! What's your favorite creature God has made?

Then, last of all, God made people just like you and me. People are God's most special creation. People can enjoy the earth and the sky and the stars and all the creatures God made. People can love God.

God looked at the people he made and said, "That's *very* good!"

Noah's Boat

(From Genesis 6–8)

Noah was a good man. He obeyed God, and that made God very happy. What do you look like when you're happy? All the other people who lived in Noah's time didn't obey God. That made God very sad. What do you look like when you're sad?

God decided to send a flood to cover the whole earth. But he wanted to save Noah and his family. So he told Noah to build a big, huge boat. The boat would have to be big enough for Noah, his family, and two of every kind of animal on earth.

Imagine what it would be like if all the animals at the zoo were on one boat. How long do you think it would take to build a boat that big?

Noah obeyed God and started building the boat. The people who didn't obey God laughed at Noah—they thought he was silly to build a boat where there was no water.

But Noah went right on building. Pound, pound, bang, bang, clackety-clack, ping. Pound, pound, bang, bang, clack-ety-clack, ping. Noah kept on hammering until the boat was done.

Then God told Noah to take his family into the boat. Then all the animals marched in, two by two. Let's march our fingers up to the boat. When everyone was in the boat, God closed the door.

Soon it started to rain. Plip, plop, drip, drop. Plip, plop, drip, drop. Let's pat our knees to make rain sounds. It rained harder and harder, but Noah and his family were safe and dry on the boat.

If you were on the boat with all those animals, which one would you pet first? A gangly giraffe? A leathery lizard? A wiggly worm?

It rained all day and all night. It kept raining and raining for days. It rained for more than a month! What do you like to do when it rains? What do you think Noah and his family did?

The water kept rising and rising, until it cov-ered the whole earth. Noah looked and looked for dry land, but all he could see was water, water, water! Let's look around and see if we see any dry land.

Finally, the rain stopped. The boat floated for days and days, weeks and weeks, months and months! Then one day, it bumped into a mountain top—KA-BUMP! Noah looked for dry land again. This time he found it!

Noah opened a window and sent out a dove. The dove couldn't find a place to make a nest, so it came back to the boat. A few days later, Noah sent out the dove again. That night, the dove came back with a leaf in its mouth. That meant trees were starting to grow. A few more days later, Noah sent out the dove once more. This time it didn't come back because it found a place to make a nest.

"Noah," God said, "You and your family and all the animals can get out of the boat."

Yea! Let's clap! Noah's family danced for joy as they left the boat. They each took a big, deep breath of fresh air. They curled their toes in the green grass. They praised God for the blue sky and bright sunshine. The earth was all fresh and clean!

Then came the animals. Clomp, stomp went the elephants. Slither, swish went the snakes. Hoppity-ho went the rabbits. What other animals came out of the boat? What sounds did they make?

Noah thanked God for keeping the boat safe while it rained and rained. God promised never to flood the whole earth again. Then God put a beautiful, shimmery rainbow in the sky.

What's your favorite color in a rainbow? Every time we see a rainbow, we can remember God's promise.

Noah was glad that he obeyed God. We can obey God, too. And God will take care of us, just like he took care of Noah.

15

The Tower That Flopped

(From Genesis 11:1-9)

16

Noah's family grew and grew,
and spread across the land.
(*Spread arms.*)
They all spoke just one language.
Everyone could understand.

Then people in a city said,
"Let's make a plan together.
We'll build a tower to the sky—
(*Move fists, one on top of the other.*)
the tallest tower ever!

"We'll build right up to heaven.
Our tower will be first-rate.
(*Thumbs up.*)
We won't need God to help us out
because <u>we</u> are so great!"
(*Take a bow.*)

So as they worked and climbed and built,
they never thought of God.
They dreamt of their great tower.
(*Clasp hands and look up.*)

17

Now don't you think that's odd?

Well, all this made God very sad.
He shook his head and thought, "Too bad!
(Shake head "no.")
They need to know I'm #1—
(Hold up one finger.)
not who they are or what they've done."

Then all at once God had a plan.
(Point finger to head.)
He'd change their language—then, oh, man!
Whatever words the people said,
the listeners would just scratch their heads.
(Scratch head.)

"Huh?" "What?" "We don't get it."
"What'd you say?" "Oh, just forget it!"
"Blabber, blabber, blooper tress!"
All their words were one big mess.
(Shrug shoulders.)

One said, "Help me lift this load."
Instead his friend hopped like a toad.
(Make one hand hop.)
Someone else asked for a drink.
  The person nearby said, "Pew, you stink!"
    (Hold your nose.)

18

This mix-up caused their plans to stop.
Their tower just became a flop.
(Thumbs down.)
The people scattered far and wide
because of silly, foolish pride.

God reigns in heaven over all.
(Make an arc with one hand.)
He makes nations rise and fall.
God deserves our thanks and praise.
(Make praying hands.)
So let's serve him all our days!

The Favorite Son

(From Genesis 37; 41; 45)

Fathers, brothers, sisters, mothers.
Me, my cat, my dog, and others.
Grandmas, uncles, aunts, and cousins.
Family members by the dozens.
How many people live with you?
Eleven or 12, or one or two?

Joseph lived with many others.
Joseph had 11 brothers!
(Count on fingers.)
Brothers Levi, Asher, Dan,
Judah, Gad, and Simeon.
Reuben, Issachar, Benjamin.
Naphtali, and Zebulun.
But Joseph was the favorite son—
his father Jacob's #1.
(Hold up one finger.)

Jacob gave his son a coat.
A brand new coat—then
he could gloat.
Purple, yellow, pink, and
green—
the prettiest coat you've ever
seen.
Joseph had more than
the others—
there were no coats for
his brothers.

The other brothers made a fuss.
"Why does he get more than us?"
They began to grumble and pout.
(Make a sour face.)
"Why did father leave us out?"

One night Joseph had a dream—
his brothers all bowed down to him!
The older boys had had enough,
so they decided to get rough.
(Hold up fists.)
"This favorite son has got to go!
Then maybe Dad will love us, too."

The boys threw Joseph in a well.
(Look down.)
Then decided they would tell
old Jacob that his son had died.
That would fix young Joseph's pride!
Then a caravan came by.
The boys said, "Hey—why don't we try
To sell our brother for some money?
Joseph a slave! Isn't that funny?

(Hold your stomach and laugh.)

His brothers got him in a mess,
but Joseph chose to try his best.
And all along he thought, "You'll see—
(Point upward.)
the Lord my God will set me free."

Even when Joseph was a slave,
he was kind and smart and brave.
Then someone nasty told a tale,
and Joseph ended up in jail!
(Wrap hands around imaginary bars.)
But still he didn't moan or pout—
he trusted God to work things out.

One day Joseph got a call
To see King Pharaoh in his hall.
(Make a crown with your hands.)
The king was troubled by his dreams.
He said, "Please tell me what this means."
Joseph helped him understand
that God in heaven had a plan.

"For seven years you'll have good crops,
(Thumbs up.)
But after that, the growing stops.
(Thumbs down.)
Get someone to make a plan
to save up all the food you can."
The king said, "Joseph, you're my man!
(Point.)
I'll make you second in command."

Now that Joseph was in charge,
He built new barns that were quite large.
(Spread arms).
He gathered food from everywhere
so there would be enough to share.
Then when the ground grew hard and dry,
people came to him to buy.

Joseph's brothers came one day.
They traveled there from far away
To get some food for their empy bowls
(Cup empty hands.)
and stop their stomachs' hungry growls.

22

(Rub stomach.)

As they bowed before their brother,
(Bow down.)
they mistook him for another.

They didn't see him as the one
who'd been their father's favorite son.
So Joseph tested them to find
(Rub your chin.)
if their hearts were mean or kind.

Joseph's brothers passed the test.
He knew they wanted what was best.
Joseph hugged them, one by one,
(Give hugs.)
and then before the day was done,
he filled their baskets with good food.
(Circle arms like a basket.)
More and more—they overflowed!

When Joseph's brothers went to pack,
(Wave goodbye.)
they promised to bring their father back.
The family moved to Egypt, where
they lived their lives in Joseph's care.
Then their days were filled with laughter,
and they lived happily ever after.
(Fold arms and nod.)

Safe in a Basket Boat

(From Exodus 2:1-10)

Moses was a baby boy born a long time ago. A mean king ruled the land, and he wanted to kill all the baby boys. Moses' mother loved him very much and wanted to hide him from the mean king. She needed to find a safe hiding place. Where could you hide a baby? What would you do if the baby cried?

Moses' mother made a nice big basket. Then she covered the outside of the basket with sticky, icky tar. Let's put our hands in the tar. Now let's put our hands together. See how they stick? Yick!

Moses' mother set the tar-covered basket out to dry. What do you think she was making? It was a boat! A tiny boat for baby Moses.

When the basket was dry, Moses' mother tucked him safely inside. The she carried the basket to the river and set it afloat in the tall grass by the river's edge. Moses floated on the river in his own little basket boat. The water rocked him gently, side to side. Let's rock in the water with baby Moses.

Moses' big sister, Miriam, hid nearby and watched the basket boat to make sure baby Moses was safe. Let's peek through the tall grass with Miriam. Someone else was watching Moses, too. Do you know who it was? God was watching Moses.

Some women came down to the river to wash. One of them was the king's daughter—a princess! Let's pretend we're washing in the water. I'll rub on some soap. Now it's your turn. Look! Is that a boat?

The princess sent a servant to find out what was moving in the tall grass that grew at the edge of the river. The servant brought the basket to the princess. What do you think the princess's face looked like when she opened the basket and found a baby boy inside? She must have been very surprised!

Miriam saw the princess holding baby Moses and ran over to her. Miriam asked, "Would you like me to find someone to take care of this baby for you?"

"Yes," answered the princess.

Who do you think Miriam found to take care of Moses? She brought back Moses' own mother! The princess told Moses' mother, "Take this baby and nurse him for me, and I will pay you."

How do you think Moses' mother felt knowing that Moses would be safe? Moses' mother was so happy to see her baby boy!

God had a special plan for Moses to keep him safe. God can keep you safe, too.

The Red Sea Run

(From Exodus 14:10-31)

Let's pretend we're Moses and the Israelites. We want to get out of Egypt—FAST!

Here we go!
We need a way to escape.
Let's run. (*Pretend to run and pant.*)
Look behind you! (*Turn and look behind.*)
Oh, no!
Here comes Pharaoh's army! (*Slap hands on thighs like galloping horses.*)
Yikes! We're scared! Keep running! (*Pretend to run and pant.*)

Now look ahead! (*Hand over eyebrows scouting ahead.*)
Oh, no! Water!
Just one big sea of water.
Nowhere to run.
Nowhere to hide.

Help us, God! (*Fold hands in prayer.*)
What should we do?
We're trapped. We can't swim!
We can't fight an army!
We're scared.

God, we need you.

Stop. *(Stop running and stand still.)*
Watch Moses.
He's lifting his staff,
that great big stick. *(Pretend to lift a heavy stick.)*
Whoa!
See what God is doing?
What's happening?
The water just split in half,
like this! *(Bring arms forward, then open wide.)*
Swoosh!
Whoosh!
Now we've got a place to run!

Come on!
Let's go between the
water walls. *(Pretend to run.)*
Yea!
We made it across the watery sea,
high and dry as dry can be!
Whoopee!

Oh, no!
Look behind you! *(Turn and look behind.)*
Here they come!
The soldiers in their chariots
want to use our dry path, too. *(Slap thighs to make sounds of approaching horses.)*
But God won't let them catch us.
No! They can't hurt us.

Look!
The water is falling!
It's swooshing back together again. *(Bring widened arms back together.)*
There's no more dry path.
It's a watery sea.
Hooray! *(Clap and cheer.)*
God won't let the soldiers get us!
We're safe!
We don't have to worry.
God will take care of us!

Thanks, God! You're great!

(*Hold arms up in praise.*)
You opened the sea to let us through.
There's no one else as great as you!

OPTIONAL: Let's dance! (*Hold hands and dance in a circle as Miriam did.*)

Shout! Shout! They All Fell Down!

(From Joshua 6:1-20)

Show me how you march. Pick your feet up high. Good!

God once helped his people by having them march like you just did. Joshua was leading God's people through a dry, dusty desert to the Promised Land. Let's blow away the dust from our path.

God's people had been looking for a long time to find the Promised Land. They knew it would be a wonderful place. What's a wonderful place you love to go to?

Joshua knew that the people who lived in the

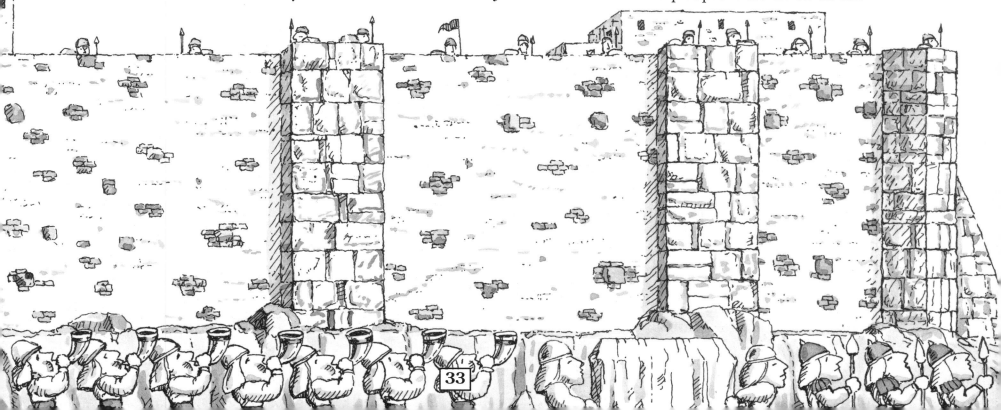

Promised Land might not want God's people to come there. Joshua was a brave leader who trusted God. Joshua knew that God would help his people go into the Promised Land.

One day, they came to Jericho, a city with BIG walls. Let's stretch up as tall as we can and try to peek over the walls. The walls were so big, not even the tallest person could see inside. How would you try to get inside a city like that?

God told Joshua, "March around the city walls every morning for six days. On the seventh day, march around the city seven times and have seven priests blow seven trumpets. After the trumpets blast, have all the people give a loud shout." Let's give a shout together. Let's shout "Hooray!"

Let's pretend we're God's people waking up and getting ready to march.

People of God! It's time to go!
Today we march around Jericho.

We're marching one, we're marching two.
Soon we'll see what God will do.

We're marching three, we're marching four.
They'll never let us in the door!

We're marching five and six and seven.
God is watching up in heaven.

Blow the trumpet loud and clear.
The Lord Jehovah is with us here!

Doodely-doodely-doot-doo-doo!
I can give a shout. Can you?

Deedely-deedely-deet-dee-dee!
Shout your favorite shout with me.

The seventh time they marched around,

those great big walls came roaring down!

Rocks and boulders tumbled away.
The people of God had won the day.
Let's shout, "Hooray for God! Hooray!"

Ruth Moves to a New Home

(From Ruth 1–4)

Naomi was a kind old woman who had two sons. One son married Ruth. The other son married Orpah. Then a sad thing happened. Naomi's husband died, then both of her sons died. That left Naomi, Ruth, and Orpah alone, with no sons or husbands.

Naomi decided it was best to move back to Bethlehem, her old home. Ruth and Orpah cried because they loved her very much. Do you get sad when people move away?

Orpah decided to stay behind, but Ruth said, "I'll go with you wherever you go." So Ruth and Naomi packed

their things and started on their journey. Let's pretend our fingers are Ruth and Naomi and walk them up hills and down hills to a new place. It was a long walk!

Where do you like to walk? What would it be like to walk all the way to a different country?

When Ruth and Naomi arrived at Bethlehem, all Naomi's friends were excited to see her. They gave her lots of hugs. Do you have a hug for me? Then Naomi explained how sad she felt because her husband and sons had died.

One day, Ruth said, "I'll go into the fields and gather the grain the farm workers leave behind. Maybe they will be kind and share their leftover grain with us."

So Ruth went to a nearby farm. After the workers picked the grain, they let Ruth pick up the leftovers. Let's pretend to pick up grain and put it in a basket.

Soon the owner of the field came and saw Ruth. He was very kind to her and let her take all the grain she needed. And he let her eat with his workers at mealtime. He said, "You are taking good care of Naomi, your mother-in-law. May God bless you for all you have done."

That night, as Naomi ate the grain Ruth brought, Naomi asked, "Who let you take all this grain?"

"The farmer's name is Boaz," Ruth answered. "He said I could work in his fields all through harvest."

"God bless Boaz!" Naomi exclaimed. "He belongs to my family. Maybe he will take care of us."

One day, Naomi told Ruth to dress up and go see Boaz. Let's pretend we're getting dressed up. Let's put on our best clothes. Now we'll spray on some perfume. There! Now we're ready to see Boaz.

When Boaz saw Ruth, he promised to take care of her. "Everyone knows what a good person you are," he said. Then Boaz talked to the other people in his family. They agreed that Boaz should marry Ruth.

The wedding was a happy day for everyone. Let's hum a wedding march for Ruth and Boaz. Have you ever been to a wedding? What was the best part?

About a year after the wedding, Ruth had a baby boy. All Naomi's friends clapped their hands and said, "God has given you a grandson and a wonderful daughter who loves you!" Let's clap our hands with Naomi and her friends.

The little boy was named Obed. When little Obed grew up, he had a son named Jesse.

When Jesse grew up, he had a son named David. David killed the giant Goliath and became the king of Israel. So Naomi became the great-great-grandmother of a king!

After all their sadness, God gave Ruth and Naomi a happy family. Sometimes sad things happen to us, too. But God can make everything turn out for the best.

A Call in the Middle of the Night

(From 1 Samuel 3:1-20)

SAMUEL

SAMUEL

SAMUEL

Samuel was a little boy who lived in the temple. It was kind of like living at church. A kind old priest named Eli took care of Samuel. One night, Samuel was in his bed, trying to go to sleep. Then he heard something. What noises do you hear when you're trying to go to sleep?

Let's pretend we're in bed like Samuel was. I'll tuck you in. Now pretend you're asleep. Just when

Samuel was about to fall asleep, he heard a call.

Let's practice listening. Keep your eyes closed. I'll whisper something, and if you hear me, raise your hand. *(Whisper the name of your child or children three times.)* Now you may open your eyes.

At first, Samuel didn't know who was calling him. He thought it was Eli, the priest. I'll pretend to be Eli. Every time you hear me say "Samuel," pop up and say, "Here I am!"

Samuel.

(Here I am.)

I did not call you.

Samuel.

(Here I am.)

I did not call you.

Samuel.

(Here I am.)

I did not call you, but go back

and lie down. When you hear your name again, say, "I'm listening, Lord."

Let's go back to bed. Close your eyes and pretend to be asleep again. The next time I say "Samuel," what will you say?

Samuel.

(I'm listening, Lord.)

Now open your eyes. After Samuel answered, the voice kept talking. Who do you think that voice came from? It came from God!

God was angry because Eli's sons had done bad things. God wanted Samuel to give that message to Eli. In the morning, Samuel woke up and got out of bed. He was afraid to tell Eli what God had said.

Have you ever been afraid to tell someone bad news? What did you do?

Even though Samuel was scared, he came when Eli called him. Samuel was brave and told Eli what God had said. Samuel obeyed God even though it was hard. When Samuel grew up, God made him an important leader. God could trust Samuel to listen and obey him.

When is it hard for you to obey God?

Let's pray and ask God to help us obey him even when it's scary or hard.

Round, Round, Tumble Down

(From 1 Samuel 17)

A time long ago in a land far away,
Israel's king was filled with dismay.
(Put hands to cheeks.)
He said, "That Goliath, the fighting machine,
has worried my troops. Oh, he's awfully mean.

"He's taller than buildings, he's taller than trees!
(Look and point up.)
I feel like I only come up to his knees.
Each day he comes out with his heavy,
bronze spear
(Cup hands around mouth.)
and shouts out loud insults the whole world
can hear.

"Morning and evening, day in and day out,
  he bothers my army with teasing and shouts.

'Why won't you fight me?' he asks. 'Are you scared?
Send out your best man! Come fight, if you dare!' "

The king told his men, "This is really not funny.
I'm willing to offer a whole lot of money
to be rid of that giant—now who'll volunteer?"
The king's men just looked at him, shaking
with fear.

"You can marry my daughter and live life tax-free
if you kill that mean giant and bring him to me."
But the soldiers replied, "We won't fight him at all.
(Shake your head.)
No prize is worth facing a giant that tall!"

Just then the boy David came into the camp.
  Who would've guessed that he'd come out
    the champ?

For David the shepherd was smaller than others.
He was sent to the camp with some food for
his brothers.

"What's happened?" he asked as he shared
cheese and bread.
(Pretend to pass out food.)
"Why are the king's soldiers' eyes filled
with dread?"
"A giant," they said, "has dared us to fight.
He called us bad names and bragged of his might."

David said to the soldiers, "I'll go and I'll fight.
(Put up fists.)
He's made fun of God—I know that's not right."
The king said, "Not you! You're only a boy!
You're no match for the giant you say
you'll destroy."

But David replied, "When my sheep are attacked
by lions or bears, I don't run—I fight back.
I know God protects me from dangers unseen.
(Fold arms and look up.)

And the Lord God will save me from
this Philistine."

The king gave his armor to make David strong.
(Flex muscles.)
But the shield was too big, and the sword was
too long.
With each step he took, the king's helmet
would rattle.
He'd surely fall down if he wore that to battle.

David looked at the armor all polished and shiny.
(Pretend to polish armor.)
But the armor was huge, and David was tiny.
Now how do you feel in too-big-for-you clothes?
That's probably how David felt, too, I suppose.

David took off the armor and went to the brook,
stuck in his hand and took a good look.
Instead of the armor, he picked up five stones.
(pretend to pick up stones)
He put one in his sling and then went out alone.

He whirled 'round that sling and then let the
stone fly.
(Pretend to twirl a sling.)
It shot like a rocket up into the sky.
And when that small stone hit the giant's
huge head,
Goliath fell down to the ground—he was dead!

When the Philistines saw that young David
had won,
they picked up their weapons and started
to run.
News of the victory soon spread all around.
(Cup hands around mouth.)
Young David was known as a hero
in town.

Young David won, even though he
was small.
With God, giants fall with no trouble at all.
(Point finger up.)
So if you have big problems troubling you,
trust in the Lord—for he'll get you through.

Elijah and the Ravens

(From 1 Kings 17:1-6)

Once, long ago, there lived a man named Elijah. Elijah was a prophet who gave people messages from God. There was a wicked king named Ahab in the land where Elijah lived. Elijah said to the wicked king, "It will not rain in this land until I say it can rain." God wanted to teach the wicked king a lesson.

God didn't let any rain fall for a long, long time. All the rivers and lakes dried up, and there was no water for the farmers. What happens to plants when it doesn't rain? Pretend you're a plant without any water.

There wasn't enough water for food to grow. The rivers dried up and the whole land turned brown. The people began to get very thirsty. What do you look like when you're thirsty?

God told Elijah where to find a stream that hadn't dried up. So Elijah walked and walked until he found the stream. It was right where God said it would be!

Elijah got down on his hands and knees and took a big drink of water from the stream. Let's pretend we're drinking water from a stream. How would you get the water in your mouth?

Elijah was glad to finally get a drink. But he was hungry, too. What does your tummy say when you're hungry? Where do you get food when you're hungry?

Elijah didn't have a refrigerator, a cupboard, or any place to buy hamburgers or pizza. Elijah was all alone in the middle of the desert, with no food. But God knew Elijah was hungry.

Early the next morning, God sent out a pair of shiny, black ravens with meat and bread in their beaks. They swooped down to the ground and landed next to Elijah. Then they opened their

beaks and gave Elijah the bread and meat. Elijah
patted the birds' heads to thank them. Then
Elijah prayed. Let's bow our heads and pray, too.
  "Thank you, God," Elijah said,
  "for always knowing where I am
  and what I need,
  and for always taking care of me.
  Amen."

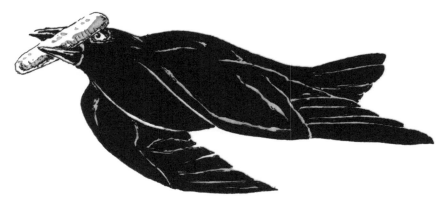

Then the ravens flew away. When
evening came, the ravens appeared again.
Once more Elijah prayed.
  "Thank you, God,
  for always knowing where I am
  and what I need,
  and for always taking care of me.
  Amen."

God sent the ravens every morning and every night with food for Elijah. And God kept water running in the little stream.

God gave Elijah what he needed, and he'll give us what we need, too. Let's say Elijah's prayer together to thank God for taking care of us.

"Thank you, God,
for always knowing where I am
and what I need,
and for always taking care of me.
Amen."

A Brave Queen

(From Esther 1–9)

A long time ago, the king of Persia gave a party. The king told the queen to come to the party. But the queen said no. If a king gave you an order, would you say no? The king was so angry that he decided to find a new queen. What do you think a queen should be like?

A Jewish man named Mordecai worked at the palace. When he heard that the king had decided to look for a new queen, he thought of his cousin Esther. Esther was

53

beautiful, kind, and brave. Best of all, she loved God.

"Esther would be a perfect queen," Mordecai thought. So Esther came to the palace with lots of other young women. When it came time for the king to choose his new queen, he chose Esther! Let's bow to the new queen.

An evil man named Haman also worked at the palace. Haman got mad at Mordecai. So one day, Haman said to the king, "The Jewish people are troublemakers. Let's make a law commanding people to kill all the Jews." The king trusted Haman, so he agreed.

Haman thought, "With this new law, I'll be able to kill Mordecai." Then he laughed an evil laugh. Let's laugh like Haman did. Ooo—I don't like Haman, do you?

But there was something Haman didn't know: Queen Esther was Jewish, too. Mordecai sent a message to Queen Esther and told her all about wicked Haman's plan. Esther was scared! What makes you scared?

But Esther was also very brave. So she sent a message back to Mordecai. It said, "Please have all the Jewish people pray for me."

So for three days and nights, Esther and the Jewish people prayed. They didn't even stop to eat. Then Esther went in to see the king.

She said, "My king, please come to a dinner I will prepare for you and Haman." What food would you fix for a king?

So the king and Haman went to Esther's dinner.

"What do you want?" the king asked. "Just tell me, and I will give it to you."

"Please come to another dinner tomorrow night. Then I'll tell you what I want," Queen Esther replied.

The next night, the king and Haman came to Esther's dinner. Again the king asked, "What do you want? Just tell me, and I will give it to you."

Esther answered, "Please let me and my people live. Someone has given the order to kill us."

"Who has done such a terrible thing?" the king thundered.

"It's Haman," Esther said, pointing at her other dinner guest.

The king was very angry. That very night he put Haman to death, for the king loved his queen and didn't want anyone to harm her. The next day, the king gave orders for the Jewish people to destroy anyone who tried to hurt them.

And that is how a brave queen saved the day. You can be strong and brave, too, and God will help you just as he helped Queen Esther.

The Fiery Furnace

(From Daniel 3:1-30)

There once was a king with a silly, long name. His name was Nebuchadnezzar. I told you it was silly!

Can you say that name with me? Nebuchadnezzar. Now let's say it three times fast. Nebuchadnezzar. Nebuchadnezzar. Nebuchadnezzar.

One day, Nebuchadnezzar woke up with a most ridiculous idea. Listen carefully, and I'll tell you about it.

When the king awoke, he said, "I think I'll make a god. I'll make it a god of gold! And I'll make it very, very tall. Everyone will have to look up to see it."

Let's look up. What do you see? Nebuchadnezzar wanted his people to look up and see a god of gold.

Is our God made of gold? No! I don't think Nebuchadnezzar had such a good idea, do you?

"And that's not all," thought Nebuchadnezzar. "When special music starts to play, all my people will kneel and worship this god of gold."

Would you want to bow to a statue? I wouldn't either.

"Anyone who doesn't bow to my god of gold will get thrown into a fiery furnace," the king declared.

Three Jewish men lived in they land. Their names were Shadrach (SHAD-rack), Meshach (ME-shack), and Abednego (uh-BED-ne-go). They worshiped the true God who made all the heavens and earth and everything in them.

"This statue made of gold is no god," they said. "And we won't worship it."

What did the king say would happen to people who didn't worship the statue? That's right—they'd be thrown into a fiery furnace. Shadrach, Meshach, and Abednego knew that. But they were very brave. Listen to what happened.

"We'll only bow to our true God, who watches us from heaven.
Let the king do what he wants—we're not scared of his oven!"

The king said, "Bow and worship this god. Let the music fill the air!"
Everyone else bowed down in fear, the but three men didn't care.

The great king roared with anger when the three men didn't bow.
"I'll teach you a thing or two. Worship my god right now.

"I told you to bow, and if you won't, I'll turn you into ash.
I'll throw you in, I'll burn you up, I'll roast you in a flash!

"Now you know what you must do. What do you have to say?"
The three men smiled, shook their heads, and bravely said, "No way."

The king's men built a flaming fire that sizzled and cracked and flared.
But Shadrach, Meshach, and Abednego didn't even look scared.

"Throw them in!" the king cried out. "Let's watch them melt away."
The soldiers pitched the three men in, but God saved the day.

For when the king looked in the flames, he couldn't believe his eyes.
"Instead of three men, I see four!" he shouted in surprise.

"Who is that fourth man in the fire—some mysterious stranger?
An angel sent by their great God to protect these men from danger?

"They're walking around, not burning up," the king just shook his head.
"By now they should be burned to a crisp and absolutely dead."

The king called out with a very loud shout—
his heart was filled with fear.
"O, servants of the most high God, come out
and talk to me here."

Out of the furnace the three men came, safe as
safe can be.
Not one little hair on their heads was burned,
for God had saved all three.

The king stepped up and shouted aloud,
"Yours is the God I'll praise.
For no other God can save like this—
I'll worship him all my days.

"From this day forward, I
declare, I'll punish any wrong
against your God who proved today
he's real and very strong."

59

The Quietest Lions Around

(From Daniel 6:1-28)

Darius was crowned king at age sixty-two.
(Use hands to make a crown.)
I think that's old for a king, how 'bout you?
The king needed helpers to rule all the land,
so he looked for some wise men to lend him
a hand.
(Strike a thoughtful pose.)

Darius chose helpers—a hundred and twenty
He thought a hundred and twenty was plenty!
(Hold arms out wide.)
He picked out three men who would help him
the most.
Daniel was named to the #1 post.
(Hold up one finger.)

Daniel was glad to advise the new king.
With wisdom from God, he could solve anything!
(Point upward, then to your head.)
So under his window each morning and night,
Daniel prayed and asked God to help him do right.
(Fold your hands.)

The king's other helpers were greedy, mean fellas.
(Rub your hands together.)
Having Daniel in charge of things made them
all jealous.
They waited for Daniel to do something wrong;
(Look at your watch.)
never has anyone waited so long!

They stormed and they stewed and they thought
night and day.
They'd get Daniel in trouble—there must be a way!
(Scratch head in thought.)
They thought and they thought, then one said
with a nod,
(Nod and make a mean face.)
"Let's get him in trouble for praying to God!

"We'll make a new law! Here's what it will say:
People must pray to the king when they pray.
(Pretend to write on your hand.)
We'll get him to sign with the seal of his ring.
Not a word can be changed. Not a bit! Not a thing!"

King Darius was flattered to hear this new deal.
(Cross your arms, smile, and nod.)
He gladly approved it with his royal seal.
(Press your ring finger into the other hand.)
He was, after all, supreme ruler and king
and could tell all his subjects to do anything.

As soon as King Darius signed the new law,
they went after Daniel, and here's what they saw:
Daniel was in his house, down on his knees
(Fold your hands and look up.)
praying to God, just as bold as you please!

They dragged faithful Daniel off to the king
and said, "He's been doing a terrible thing—
(Point accusingly.)
praying to God! Now don't you forget—
the law says he must be thrown into the pit.
(Point downward.)

There was no way that Darius could save
his adviser.
He said sadly, "Daniel, I should have been wiser!
(Shake your head.)
I shouldn't have listened to those evil men;
may your God protect you in that lions' den!"

The king woke the next morning and jumped
out of bed,
threw his robe 'round his shoulders, his crown

on his head.
(Pretend to put on a robe and crown.)
He threw open the doors and flew from his room.
(Pretend to open doors and run.)
He had to find out what had happened—and soon!

As fast as he could, the king ran to the den,
sure that the lions had eaten his friend.
He stopped, looked, and listened, but heard not
a sound.
(Look around and cup hands to ears.)
Those cats were the quietest lions around!

"Daniel!" he called. "Did the God that you serve
keep you from being the lions' hors d'oeuvre?"
"Yes," Daniel answered. "I prayed through
the night,
and an angel shut all of the lions' mouths tight!
(Point up, then clamp hands around head.)

"The great God I worship would never desert me;
not once did these big hungry cats try to hurt me.
(Lick your chops.)

Not a growl did I hear, not a purr, not a roar,
not a peep, not a sneeze, not a sniff, not a snore."
(Shake head.)

The king was delighted, and he gave a great shout,
(Hold up arms in victory.)
"Come here, all you servants, and pull Daniel out!"
(Beckon, then pull on imaginary ropes.)
To all of the bad guys he said, "This is it.
Now it's your turn to go down in the pit!"
(Point outward, then downward.)

Darius made up a new law right away:
(Pretend to write on hand.)
"Respect Daniel's God—he saved Daniel today!"
Then to the whole kingdom, they told
Daniel's story,
worshiped the true God, and gave him great glory!

Running Away

(From Jonah 1–4)

Once there was a prophet named Jonah, and he was in a big hurry. Let's pretend we're in a hurry, too. Pump your arms so you can go really fast.

Can you guess why Jonah was in such a hurry?

Jonah was running away! God asked Jonah to go preach to the people in Nineveh. But Jonah didn't want to go.

Show me how you look when you don't want to do something. I bet Jonah looked just like that. So instead of going to Nineveh, Jonah took off in the other direction.

Jonah thought if he ran far, far away, maybe God wouldn't find him. Do you think Jonah was right?

Jonah pushed up his sleeves and ran for the sea. Let's run with him. He panted and huffed and panted and huffed 'til he got to the shore. Then he ran right up the ramp and into a big boat. "Whew!" he said as he sat down. "I made it!"

Let's take three deep breaths with Jonah. "Whew! We made it, too!"

Jonah asked, "Where is this ship going?"

"All the way across the sea," the captain answered.

"Good," said Jonah. And he paid for a ticket.

Then Jonah went down into the lowest part of the boat and slid down behind a big box. He didn't want anyone to find him since he was running away. He curled up into a little ball so no one could see him. Let's curl up into a little ball, too.

Sh! Be very quiet. Jonah was so quiet that nobody knew he was there—well, almost nobody. Who do you think knew where Jonah was?

Finally the ship set sail. It rocked back and forth, back and forth. Let's pretend we're on the ship and it's rocking back and forth. Soon the rocking of the ship put Jonah to sleep.

All at once, the waves grew bigger. Clouds billowed in, and the wind got stronger. The boat rocked harder. What sound does the wind make?

Whoosh! Splash! Crash! The waves were so big that they splashed over the side of the boat. The sailors fell down and crashed into each other. They were getting scared the boat might sink. They started throwing things overboard to keep the boat from sinking.

Still the wind kept blowing and the boat kept rocking. The sailors were sure the boat was going to sink. The captain went down into the ship to look for Jonah. He found Jonah fast asleep.

"How can you sleep in this storm?" he shouted. "Get up and pray!"

Jonah knew the storm was blowing because of him. He was running away from God, but God knew where to find him. Jonah told the sailors, "If you throw me overboard, the storm will stop."

Jonah scrunched his eyes shut, so scrunch your eyes shut. He plugged his nose, so plug your nose. And he took a big gulp of air, so take a big gulp of air. The sailors threw Jonah overboard with a one-two-THREE! Right away the storm stopped.

Jonah hit the water with a loud "ker-PLASH!" And he sank and he sank and he sank. Before Jonah had a chance to start swimming, a huge fish swallowed him. When Jonah opened his eyes, he was in the belly of the fish. What would it be like inside a fish?

Jonah was there for three days and three nights. While he was inside, he prayed to God. What do you think he said to God?

"Lord, thank you for saving my life," Jonah prayed. "I'm sorry for running away."

God listened to Jonah's prayer and told the fish to spit Jonah out onto dry land. How do you think Jonah felt when he landed on the shore? I bet he took a big, deep gulp of fresh air. Let's do that, too.

God said, "Jonah, I want you to go the the city of Nineveh and tell the people there to start obeying me."

This time Jonah obeyed God. He jumped up and ran to Nineveh. And when he preached to the people there, they believed in God.

So...

the next time you think about running away, remember old Jonah and quickly obey.

He ended up deep inside a big fish, then learned to say, "Yes, Lord, I'll do what you wish."

Contributors

Lois Keffer
loves to write for children and plans never to grow up.

Martin Nagy
has served children and families in the roles of teacher, writer, social worker, and parent.

Amy Nappa
is a free-lance writer with an adorable preschooler named Tony.

Beth Rowland
is a gifted writer and musician who enjoys sharing her music and her faith with children.

Janice Thatcher
is a former circus performer who now works in Christian publishing.

Jennifer Root Wilger
is an editor who works in curriculum development at Group Publishing.

Christine Yount
is a creative teacher and editor who enjoys trying out her ideas on her two young children.